BEST OF
INDIA

Consultant Editor:
Valerie Ferguson

HERMES
HOUSE

Contents

Introduction   4

Spices   6

Techniques   8

Recipes

    Starters & Soups   10
    Fish & Shellfish   20
    Chicken & Meat   30
    Side Dishes & Accompaniments   44
    Desserts   58

Index   64

Introduction

Cooking Indian food has never been easier now that supermarkets are selling a wide range of unusual spices, exotic vegetables and special ingredients. The secret lies in the imaginative use of spices and aromatics, preferably freshly ground. Different cooking techniques bring out a different flavour from each spice. The combinations of flavours and varieties of tastes are endless.

You will find some well-known restaurant favourites in this book, such as Chicken Tikka, Rogan Josh, Beef Madras and King Prawn Korma, together with some more innovative dishes. India is a vast subcontinent, so the climate, produce and culinary traditions vary from north to south and from east to west. Northern cuisine features nuts, yogurt and ghee (clarified butter), while chillies are characteristic of southern dishes. Fish and hotly-spiced dishes are typical of eastern India and the west of India has incorporated many foreign culinary influences in its cuisine.

Cooking techniques vary, too, from slow-cooked curries and the slow marinating of ingredients to fast stir-frying, so that you can match your choice of recipes to the occasion and time available. In *Best of India* you will find dishes which celebrate the authentic taste of this inspiring cuisine.

Spices

It is the blending of spices, seasonings and flavourings that gives Indian food its character. The quantities specified in the recipes are merely a guide, so feel free to increase or decrease these as you wish.

CARDAMOM: These pods are green, black and creamy-beige, green being the most common. Whole pods used in rice and meat dishes to add flavour should not be eaten. Use the black seeds in desserts.

CINNAMON: It is available whole or ground. The sticks are used for flavour and are not eaten.

CLOVES: These are used in spice mixtures, such as garam masala, and in meat and rice dishes.

CORIANDER: One of the most popular spices, these small beige seeds are used whole and ground, giving a slightly sweet flavour. Coriander leaves are used for flavouring and as a garnish.

CUMIN: Available as whole dark-brown seeds and ground. The whole seeds are often fried in oil, releasing a strong musky flavour and aroma.

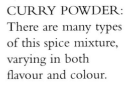

CURRY LEAVES: *Neem* leaves or *kari phulia*. These aromatic leaves are the Indian version of bay leaves.

CURRY POWDER: There are many types of this spice mixture, varying in both flavour and colour.

FENNEL SEEDS: Similar in smell and taste to aniseed, they are used in many vegetable and meat dishes. Roasted fennel seeds are also eaten after a meal, to freshen the mouth.

FENUGREEK SEEDS: These small pungent seeds are used sparingly in spice mixtures.

FRESH AND DRIED CHILLIES:
These red chillies are often fried in oil
to release their strong flavour. The
small ones are the
most pungent.
Chilli powder is
ground dried
chillies. The
strength varies,
depending on the
chilli. It is very hot
and used often.

GARAM MASALA:
This is the main
spice mixture of
Indian cooking. It
is a hot and
aromatic powder
and is added at the
end of cooking.

GINGER: Both
fresh and ground
ginger have a
sharp, refreshing
flavour. Peel fresh
root ginger
before using.

MUSTARD
SEEDS: Whole
seeds are added
to hot oil to
release a nutty
flavour. They
are used with
vegetables and pulses.

ONION SEEDS: These black and
triangular seeds are used in pickles
and to flavour vegetable curries.

PEPPERCORNS:
Black peppercorns are
used whole and
ground. They are also
used in garam masala.

SAFFRON: The
dried stigmas of the
saffron crocus are
used in savoury
and sweet dishes
for their distinctive
aroma and bright
orange colour.

TURMERIC: A bright yellow
powder, it is primarily used for its
colouring properties. Because of its
strong, bitter
flavour it
should be
used quite
sparingly.

Techniques

CRUSHING SPICES

Some spices are used whole, but where they are crushed or ground, the best flavour will be obtained if you start off with whole spices and crush them as and when needed.

1 Crush whole spices in a coffee grinder or spice mill.

2 Alternatively, use a pestle and mortar, especially for small quantities of spices.

PREPARING CHILLIES

Chillies add a distinct flavour. The seeds can be left in if a hotter result is desired.

1 Always protect your hands, as chillies can irritate the skin; wear rubber or plastic gloves and never rub your eyes after handling chillies. Halve the chilli lengthways and remove and discard the seeds.

2 Slice, finely chop and use as required. Wash the knife and board thoroughly in hot, soapy water. Always wash your hands scrupulously after preparing chillies.

Curry Powder

Makes about 115 g/4 oz

INGREDIENTS
WHOLE SPICES
50 g/2 oz/½ cup coriander seeds
60 ml/4 tbsp cumin seeds
30 ml/2 tbsp fennel seeds
30 ml/2 tbsp fenugreek seeds
4 dried red chillies
5 curry leaves

GROUND SPICES
15 ml/1 tbsp chilli powder
15 ml/1 tbsp turmeric
2.5 ml/½ tsp salt

1 Dry-roast the whole spices in a large heavy-based frying pan over medium heat for 8–10 minutes, shaking the pan, until the spices begin to darken and release a rich aroma. Allow them to cool slightly.

2 Put the spices in a coffee grinder and grind to a fine powder. Add the remaining ground spices and store in an airtight jar.

Garam Masala

Makes about 50 g/2 oz

INGREDIENTS
10 dried red chillies
3 x 2.5 cm/1 in cinnamon sticks
2 curry leaves
30 ml/2 tbsp coriander seeds
30 ml/2 tbsp cumin seeds
5 ml/1 tsp black peppercorns
5 ml/1 tsp cloves
5 ml/1 tsp fenugreek seeds
5 ml/1 tsp black mustard seeds
1.5 ml/¼ tsp chilli powder

1 Dry-roast the chillies, cinnamon sticks and curry leaves in a large heavy-based frying pan for 2 minutes.

2 Add the coriander and cumin seeds, peppercorns, cloves, fenugreek and mustard seeds and dry-roast for a further 8–10 minutes, shaking the pan, until the spices begin to darken and release a rich aroma.

3 Allow the mixture to cool slightly before grinding it to a fine powder. Add the chilli powder, mix together and store in an airtight jar.

9

Curried Lamb Samosas

These spicy, meat-filled, pastry triangles may be served as a first course or as a tasty snack at any time of day.

Serves 4

INGREDIENTS
15 ml/1 tbsp oil
1 garlic clove, crushed
175 g/6 oz/1¼ cups minced (ground) lamb
4 spring onions, finely chopped
10 ml/2 tsp medium curry paste
4 ready-to-eat dried apricots,
    chopped
1 small potato, diced
10 ml/2 tsp apricot chutney
30 ml/2 tbsp frozen peas
dash of lemon juice
15 ml/1 tbsp chopped
    fresh coriander
225 g/8 oz puff pastry
beaten egg, to glaze
5 ml/1 tsp cumin seeds
salt and freshly ground
    black pepper
fresh mint sprigs, to garnish
45 ml/3 tbsp natural yogurt and 15 ml/
    1 tbsp chopped fresh mint, to serve

1 Preheat the oven to 220°C/425°F/ Gas 7 and dampen a large, non-stick baking sheet.

2 Heat the oil in a large frying pan and fry the garlic for 30 seconds without browning, then add the minced lamb. Continue frying for about 5 minutes, stirring frequently, until the meat is well browned.

3 Stir in the spring onions, curry paste, apricots and potato and cook for 2–3 minutes. Add the apricot chutney, peas and 60 ml/4 tbsp water. Cover and simmer for 10 minutes, stirring occasionally. Stir in the lemon juice and chopped fresh coriander. Season, remove from the heat and leave to cool.

4 On a floured surface, roll out the pastry and cut into four 15 cm/ 6 in squares. Place a quarter of the curry mixture in the centre of each pastry square and brush the edges with beaten egg. Fold over to make a triangle and seal the edges. Knock up the edges with the back of a knife and make a small slit in the top of each.

5 Brush each samosa with beaten egg and sprinkle over the cumin seeds. Place on the damp baking sheet and bake for 20 minutes. Serve with yogurt and mint and garnish with mint sprigs.

Chicken Tikka

This popular appetizer can also be served as a main course for four.

Serves 6

INGREDIENTS
450 g/1 lb/3¼ cups skinless, boneless
   chicken, cubed
5 ml/1 tsp grated fresh root ginger
5 ml/1 tsp crushed garlic
5 ml/1 tsp chilli powder
1.5 ml/¼ tsp turmeric
5 ml/1 tsp salt
150 ml/¼ pint/⅔ cup natural yogurt
60 ml/4 tbsp lemon juice
15 ml/1 tbsp chopped fresh coriander
15 ml/1 tbsp vegetable oil

FOR THE GARNISH
1 small onion, cut into rings, lime wedges,
   mixed salad, fresh coriander

1 In a medium bowl, mix together the chicken pieces, ginger, garlic, chilli powder, turmeric, salt, yogurt, lemon juice and fresh coriander and leave to marinate for at least 2 hours to allow the flavours to develop.

2 Preheat the grill to medium. Place the marinated chicken pieces on a grill tray or in a flameproof dish lined with foil and baste with the oil.

3 Grill the chicken for 15–20 minutes, until cooked, turning and basting 2–3 times. Serve garnished with the onion rings, lime wedges, salad and coriander.

Kofta

Serve these tasty beef or lamb rissoles with freshly made naan and raita.

Makes 20–25

INGREDIENTS
450 g/1 lb/3 cups lean minced (ground)
  beef or lamb
30 ml/2 tbsp finely ground ginger
30 ml/2 tbsp finely ground garlic
4 green chillies, finely chopped
1 small onion, finely chopped
1 egg, lightly beaten
2.5 ml/½ tsp turmeric
5 ml/1 tsp garam masala
50 g/2 oz/1 cup coriander leaves, chopped
4–6 mint leaves, chopped or 2.5 ml/½ tsp
  mint sauce
175 g/6 oz potato
vegetable oil, for deep frying
salt

1 Place the first 10 ingredients in a large bowl and mix well so that the meat is well coated. Grate the potato into the bowl, and season with salt to taste. Knead together to blend well and form a soft dough.

2 Divide the mixture into portions the size of golf balls. Place in the fridge to rest for about 25 minutes.

3 In a wok or frying pan, heat the oil to medium hot and fry the koftas in small batches until they are golden brown in colour. Drain well on kitchen paper, keeping each batch hot in a medium oven until all the koftas are cooked. Serve hot.

Onion Bhajias

Bhajias are a classic snack of India. The same batter may be used with a variety of vegetables.

Makes 20–25

INGREDIENTS
225 g/8 oz/2 cups gram flour (*besan*)
   or *chana atta*
2.5 ml/½ tsp chilli powder
5 ml/1 tsp turmeric powder
5 ml/1 tsp baking powder
1.5 ml/¼ tsp asafoetida
2.5 ml/½ tsp each, fennel, cumin
   and onion seeds, coarsely crushed
2 large onions, finely sliced
2 green chillies, finely chopped
50 g/2 oz/1 cup coriander leaves, chopped
cold water, to mix
vegetable oil, for deep frying
salt

2 Add the coarsely-crushed seeds, onions, green chillies and coriander leaves and toss together using your hands to thoroughly coat all the ingredients. Gradually, mix in enough cold water to make a thick batter.

1 In a large bowl, sift together the gram flour (*besan*) or *chana atta*, chilli powder, turmeric, baking powder, asafoetida and salt. Raise the sieve well above the bowl to incorporate as much air as possible.

3 Heat enough oil in a *karahi* (Indian frying pan) or wok for deep-frying. Drop spoonfuls of the mixture into the hot oil and fry until they are brown. Leave enough space to turn the bhajias. Drain well and serve hot.

Tomato & Coriander Soup

Tomato soup is always popular. Serve with bread on a cold winter's day.

Serves 4

INGREDIENTS
675 g/1½ lb tomatoes
30 ml/2 tbsp vegetable oil
1 bay leaf
4 spring onions, chopped
5 ml/1 tsp salt
2.5 ml/½ tsp crushed garlic
5 ml/1 tsp crushed black peppercorns
30 ml/2 tbsp chopped fresh coriander
750 ml/1¼ pints/good 3 cups water
15 ml/1 tbsp cornflour

FOR THE GARNISH
1 spring onion, chopped (optional)
30 ml/2 tbsp single cream (optional)

1 To remove the tomato skins, briefly blanch the tomatoes in very hot water. Peel and chop the flesh. In a medium saucepan, heat the oil and fry the chopped tomatoes, bay leaf and chopped spring onions for a few minutes until soft.

2 Add the salt, garlic, peppercorns and fresh coriander, mixing well, finally adding the water. Bring to the boil, lower the heat and simmer for 15–20 minutes.

3 Dissolve the cornflour in a little water, stirring to form a smooth paste. Remove the soup from the heat and press through a strainer. Return to the pan, add the cornflour and stir over a gentle heat for about 3 minutes, until thickened.

4 Pour into individual serving dishes and garnish with the chopped spring onion and cream, if using. Serve hot with bread.

COOK'S TIP: If the only fresh tomatoes available are rather pale and underripe, add 15 ml/1 tbsp tomato purée to the pan with the chopped tomatoes to enhance the colour and flavour of the soup.

Spiced Cauliflower Soup

Light and tasty, this creamy, mildly spicy soup is multi-purpose. It makes a wonderful warming first course or an appetizing quick meal.

Serves 4–6

INGREDIENTS
1 large potato, peeled and diced
1 small cauliflower, chopped
1 onion, chopped
15 ml/1 tbsp sunflower oil
1 garlic clove, crushed
15 ml/1 tbsp grated fresh root ginger
10 ml/2 tsp ground turmeric
5 ml/1 tsp cumin seeds
5 ml/1 tsp black mustard seeds
10 ml/2 tsp ground coriander
1 litre/1¾ pints/4 cups vegetable stock
300 ml/½ pint/1¼ cups natural yogurt
salt and freshly ground black pepper
fresh coriander or parsley, to garnish

1 Put the potato, cauliflower and onion into a large saucepan with the oil and 45 ml/3 tbsp water. Heat until hot and bubbling, then cover and lower the heat to a gentle simmer. Continue cooking the mixture for about 10 minutes.

2 Add the garlic, ginger and spices. Stir well and cook for a further 2 minutes, stirring occasionally. Pour in the stock and season well with salt and pepper. Bring to the boil, then cover and simmer for about 20 minutes. Stir in the yogurt, adjust the seasoning if necessary and garnish with coriander or parsley.

Dhal Soup

This is a simple, filling, mildly spiced lentil soup, which would suit a menu that also includes heavily-spiced meat dishes.

Serves 4–6

INGREDIENTS
15 ml/1 tbsp ghee
1 large onion, finely chopped
2 cloves garlic, crushed
1 green chilli, chopped
2.5 ml/½ tsp turmeric
75 g/3 oz/⅓ cup red lentils (*masoor dhal*)
250 ml/8 fl oz/1 cup water
400 g/14 oz can chopped tomatoes
2.5 ml/½ tsp sugar
lemon juice
200 g/7 oz/1 cup plain boiled rice or
   2 potatoes, boiled and cubed (optional)
salt
chopped coriander leaves, to garnish

1 Heat the ghee in a large saucepan and fry the onion, garlic, chilli and turmeric until the onion is translucent.

2 Add the lentils and water and bring to the boil. Reduce the heat, cover and cook gently until all the water is absorbed.

3 Mash the lentils with the back of a wooden spoon until you have a smooth paste. Add salt and mix well.

4 Add the remaining ingredients including the rice or cubed potatoes, if using. Serve garnished with chopped fresh coriander leaves.

Fish Curry

Any mixture of white fish works well with this fresh curry. Serve with warm naan bread to mop up the delicious juices.

Serves 4

INGREDIENTS
675 g/1½ lb white boneless fish, such as
  halibut, cod, coley or monkfish
juice of ½ lime
5 ml/2 tsp cider vinegar
225 g/8 oz/4 cups grated fresh coconut
2.5 cm/1 in piece of fresh root ginger, grated
6 garlic cloves
450 g/1 lb tomatoes, chopped
45 ml/3 tbsp sunflower oil
350 g/12 oz onions, roughly chopped
20 curry leaves
5 ml/1 tsp ground coriander
2.5 ml/½ tsp ground turmeric
300 ml/½ pint/1¼ cups water
10 ml/2 tsp ground chilli
2.5 ml/½ tsp fenugreek seeds
2.5 ml/½ tsp cumin seeds
salt and freshly ground black pepper
lime slices and grated coconut, to garnish
banana leaves, to serve (optional)

1 Put the fish in a non-metallic bowl. Add the lime juice, vinegar and salt and marinate for 30 minutes.

2 In a food processor, blend the grated coconut, ginger, garlic cloves and tomatoes.

3 Heat the oil in a frying pan, add the onions and cook until golden brown, then add the curry leaves.

4 Add the coriander, turmeric and chilli and stir-fry for 1 minute. Add the coconut paste and cook for 3–4 minutes, constantly stirring. Pour in 300 ml/½ pint/1¼ cups water, bring to the boil, and simmer for 4 minutes.

5 Pound the fenugreek and cumin seeds in a mortar with a pestle. Lay the fish on top of the sauce, sprinkle over the fenugreek mixture and cook for 15 minutes, or until the fish is tender. Carefully remove the fish and cut into pieces. Serve with the sauce on banana leaves, if using, and garnish with grated coconut and lime slices.

Fish Stew

A spicy fish stew made with potatoes, peppers and traditional Indian spices makes a filling midweek supper.

Serves 4

INGREDIENTS
30 ml/2 tbsp oil
5 ml/1 tsp cumin seeds
1 onion, chopped
1 red pepper, thinly sliced
1 garlic clove, crushed
2 red chillies, finely chopped
2 bay leaves
2.5 ml/½ tsp salt
5 ml/1 tsp ground cumin
5 ml/1 tsp ground coriander
5 ml/1 tsp chilli powder
400 g/14 oz can chopped tomatoes
2 large potatoes, cut into 2.5 cm/1 in chunks
300 ml/½ pint/1¼ cups fish stock
4 cod fillets
chapatis, to serve

1 Heat the oil in a large deep-sided frying pan and fry the cumin seeds for 2 minutes, until they begin to splutter. Add the onion, pepper, garlic, chillies and bay leaves and stir well.

2 Fry the vegetables for 5–7 minutes on a low heat, until the onions have browned.

3 Add the salt, ground cumin, ground coriander and chilli powder and cook for 3–4 minutes.

4 Stir in the tomatoes, potatoes and fish stock. Bring to the boil and simmer for a further 10 minutes.

5 Add the fish, then cover and simmer for 10 minutes, or until the fish is tender. Serve with chapatis.

King Prawn Korma

This korma has a mild, creamy texture and makes a good introduction to Indian cuisine for people who claim not to like spicy food.

Serves 4

INGREDIENTS
10–12 frozen cooked king prawns, thawed
45 ml/3 tbsp natural yogurt
45 ml/3 tbsp fromage frais
5 ml/1 tsp ground paprika
5 ml/1 tsp garam masala
15 ml/1 tbsp tomato purée
45 ml/3 tbsp coconut milk
5 ml/1 tsp chilli powder
150 ml/¼ pint/⅔ cup water
15 ml/1 tbsp corn oil
5 ml/1 tsp crushed garlic
5 ml/1 tsp grated fresh root ginger
½ piece cinnamon bark
2 green cardamom pods
salt
15 ml/1 tbsp chopped fresh coriander,
    to garnish

1 Drain the prawns to ensure that all excess liquid is removed and peel them, if necessary.

2 Place the yogurt, fromage frais, paprika, garam masala, tomato purée, coconut milk, chilli powder and water in a bowl. Blend everything together well and set aside.

3 Heat the oil in a non-stick wok or frying pan, add the garlic, ginger, cinnamon, cardamoms and salt to taste and fry over a low heat.

4 Pour in the yogurt and spice mixture and bring to the boil over a medium heat, stirring occasionally.

5 Add the prawns and continue to stir-fry until the sauce is quite thick. Serve garnished with the chopped coriander.

COOK'S TIP: Paprika adds a good rich colour to the curry without extra heat.

Goan-style Mussels

This is a quick and simple way to cook fresh mussels in a delicious fragrant coconut sauce. Discard any unopened mussels before serving.

Serves 4

INGREDIENTS
900 g/2 lb mussels
115 g/4 oz/2 cups creamed coconut
45 ml/3 tbsp oil
1 onion, finely chopped
3 garlic cloves, crushed
2.5 cm/1 in piece fresh root ginger,
    finely chopped
2.5 ml/½ tsp ground turmeric
5 ml/1 tsp ground cumin
5 ml/1 tsp ground coriander
1.5 ml/¼ tsp salt
chopped fresh coriander,
    to garnish

3 Heat the oil in a large pan and fry the onion for 5 minutes. Add the garlic and ginger and fry for 2 minutes. Stir in the turmeric, cumin, coriander and salt and fry for a further 2 minutes. Add the creamed coconut liquid, bring to the boil and simmer for 5 minutes.

1 Scrub the mussels under cold, running water and remove the beards. Discard any mussels that do not shut when sharply tapped.

2 Dissolve the creamed coconut in 450 ml/¾ pint/1¾ cups boiling water and set aside until needed.

4 Add the mussels, cover and cook for 6–8 minutes, or until all the mussels are cooked and open. Spoon the mussels on to a serving platter with the sauce, then garnish with the chopped fresh coriander.

Balti Prawns in Hot Sauce

This sizzling prawn dish is cooked in a fiery hot sauce. If the heat is too much, serving with raita will soften the piquant flavour.

Serves 4

INGREDIENTS
2 medium onions, roughly chopped
30 ml/2 tbsp tomato purée
5 ml/1 tsp ground coriander
1.5 ml/¼ tsp turmeric
5 ml/1 tsp chilli powder
2 medium fresh green chillies
45 ml/3 tbsp chopped fresh coriander
30 ml/2 tbsp lemon juice
5 ml/1 tsp salt
45 ml/3 tbsp corn oil
16 cooked king prawns, peeled
1 fresh green chilli, chopped (optional)

2 Heat the oil in a deep round-bottomed frying pan or a *karahi*. Lower the heat slightly and add the spice mixture. Fry the mixture for 3–5 minutes, or until the sauce has thickened slightly.

1 Put the onions, tomato purée, ground coriander, turmeric, chilli powder, 2 whole green chillies, 30 ml/ 2 tbsp of the fresh coriander, lemon juice and salt into a food processor. Process for about 1 minute. If the mixture seems too thick, add a little water to loosen it.

3 Add the prawns and stir-fry quickly over a medium heat. As soon as the prawns are heated through, transfer them to a serving dish and garnish with the rest of the fresh coriander and the chopped green chilli, if using. Serve immediately.

Tandoori Chicken

The chicken is marinated the night before, so all you have to do on the day is to cook it in a very hot oven.

Serves 4

INGREDIENTS
1 x 1.75 kg/4-4½ lb chicken,
    cut into 8 pieces
juice of 1 large lemon
150 ml/¼ pint/⅔ cup natural yogurt
3 garlic cloves, crushed
30 ml/2 tbsp olive oil
5 ml/1 tsp ground turmeric
10 ml/2 tsp ground paprika
5 ml/1 tsp grated fresh root ginger
    or 2.5 ml/½ tsp ground ginger
10 ml/2 tsp garam masala
5 ml/1 tsp salt
a few drops of red food colouring (optional)
Salad leaves and lemon wedges, to garnish

2 Mix together the remaining ingredients and pour the sauce over the chicken pieces, turning them to coat thoroughly. Cover with clear film and chill in the fridge overnight.

1 Remove the skin from the chicken pieces and cut two slits in each piece. Arrange the chicken in a single layer in an ovenproof dish and pour over the lemon juice, turning the chicken to coat well.

3 Preheat the oven to 220°C/425°F/ Gas 7. Remove the chicken from the marinade and arrange in a single layer on a shallow baking tray. Bake for 15 minutes, turn over and cook for a further 15 minutes, or until tender.

Chicken Korma

A korma is a rich creamy dish from northern India. This recipe uses a combination of yogurt and cream.

Serves 4

INGREDIENTS
675 g/1½ lb skinless chicken breasts
25 g/1 oz/¼ cup blanched almonds
2 garlic cloves, crushed
2.5 cm/1 in piece fresh root ginger,
    roughly chopped
30 ml/2 tbsp oil
3 green cardamom pods
1 onion, finely chopped
10 ml/2 tsp ground cumin
1.5 ml/¼ tsp salt
150 ml/¼ pint/⅔ cup natural yogurt
175 ml/6 fl oz/¾ cup single cream
toasted flaked almonds and a fresh coriander
    sprig, to garnish
plain rice, to serve

3 Heat the oil in a large frying pan and cook the chicken for 8–10 minutes, or until browned. Remove with a slotted spoon. Drain on kitchen paper and set aside.

4 Add the cardamom pods and fry for 2 minutes. Add the onion and fry for a further 5 minutes.

5 Stir in the almond and garlic paste, cumin and salt and cook for a further 5 minutes, stirring to blend the flavours.

1 Using a sharp knife, cut the chicken into 2.5 cm/1 in cubes.

2 Put the almonds, garlic and ginger into a food processor or blender with 30 ml/2 tbsp water and process to a smooth paste.

6 Add the yogurt gradually and cook over a low heat until it has all been absorbed. Return the chicken to the pan. Cover and simmer for 5–6 minutes or until the chicken is tender. Add the cream and simmer for 5 minutes. Serve with plain rice and garnish with toasted flaked almonds and coriander.

Balti Chicken

This recipe, with its use of cardamom and cinnamon, has a beautifully delicate flavour, and is probably the most popular of all Balti dishes.

Serves 4–6

INGREDIENTS
45 ml/3 tbsp corn oil
3 medium onions, sliced
3 medium tomatoes, halved and sliced
2.5 cm/1 in cinnamon stick
2 large black cardamom pods
4 black peppercorns
2.5 ml/½ tsp black cumin seeds
5 ml/1 tsp grated fresh root ginger
5 ml/1 tsp crushed garlic
5 ml/1 tsp garam masala
5 ml/1 tsp chilli powder
5 ml/1 tsp salt
1–1.5kg/2¼–3 lb chicken, skinned and
   cut into 8 pieces
30 ml/2 tbsp natural yogurt
60 ml/4 tbsp lemon juice
30 ml/2 tbsp chopped fresh coriander
2 fresh green chillies, chopped

2 Add the cinnamon stick, cardamoms, peppercorns, black cumin seeds, ginger, garlic, garam masala, chilli powder and salt. Lower the heat and stir-fry for 3–5 minutes to bring out the flavour of the spices.

1 Heat the oil in a large karahi or deep, round-bottomed frying pan. Add the onions and fry until they are golden. Add the tomatoes and stir.

3 Add the chicken pieces, 2 at a time, and stir-fry for at least 7 minutes, or until the spice mixture has completely penetrated the chicken pieces and the chicken is cooked. Add the yogurt to the chicken and mix well.

4 Lower the heat and cover the pan with a piece of foil, making sure that the foil does not touch the food. Cook very gently for about 15 minutes, checking once to make sure the food is not catching on the bottom of the pan.

5 Finally, add the lemon juice, fresh coriander and green chillies and serve at once.

COOK'S TIP: If desired, use 675 g/ 1½ lb boned and cubed chicken.

Chicken Biryani

Biryanis originated in Persia and are traditionally made with meat and rice. They are often served on festive occasions.

Serves 4

INGREDIENTS
275 g/10 oz/1½ cups basmati rice
30 ml/2 tbsp oil
1 onion, thinly sliced
2 garlic cloves, crushed
1 green chilli, finely chopped
2.5 cm/1 in fresh root ginger,
    finely chopped
675 g/1½ lb skinless chicken breasts,
    cut into 2.5 cm/1 in cubes
45 ml/3 tbsp ready-made curry paste
1.5 ml/¼ tsp salt
1.5 ml/¼ tsp garam masala
3 tomatoes, cut into thin wedges
1.5 ml/¼ tsp ground turmeric
2 bay leaves
4 green cardamom pods
4 cloves
1.5 ml/¼ tsp saffron strands
chutney, to serve

1 Wash the rice in several changes of cold water. Put into a large bowl, cover with plenty of water and leave to soak for 30 minutes.

2 Meanwhile, heat the oil in a large frying pan and fry the onion for about 5–7 minutes, until lightly browned. Add the garlic, chilli and ginger and fry for about 2 minutes. Add the chicken and fry for about 5 minutes, stirring occasionally.

3 Add the curry paste, salt and garam masala and cook for 5 minutes. Add the tomatoes and continue to cook for a further 3–4 minutes. Remove from the heat and set aside.

4 Preheat the oven to 190°C/375°F/ Gas 5. Bring a large saucepan of water to the boil. Drain the rice and add it to the pan with the turmeric. Cook for about 10 minutes, or until the rice is almost tender. Drain the rice and toss together with the bay leaves, cardamoms, cloves and saffron.

5 Layer the cooked rice and chicken in a shallow, ovenproof dish until all the mixture has been used, finishing off with a layer of rice. Cover with a lid or foil and bake in the oven for 15–20 minutes, or until the chicken is tender when pierced with the tip of a knife. Transfer to individual plates and serve with chutney.

Rogan Josh

The lamb is marinated in yogurt, then cooked with spices and tomatoes which give the dish its rich, red appearance.

Serves 4

INGREDIENTS
900 g/2 lb lamb fillet
45 ml/3 tbsp lemon juice
250 ml/8 fl oz/1 cup natural yogurt
5 ml/1 tsp salt
2 garlic cloves, crushed
2.5 cm/1 in piece fresh root
    ginger, grated
60 ml/4 tbsp oil
2.5 ml/½ tsp cumin seeds
2 bay leaves
4 green cardamom pods
1 onion, finely chopped
10 ml/2 tsp ground coriander
10 ml/2 tsp ground cumin
5 ml/1 tsp chilli powder
400 g/14 oz can chopped tomatoes
30 ml/2 tbsp tomato purée
toasted cumin seeds and bay leaves,
    to garnish
plain rice, to serve

1 With a sharp knife, trim away any excess fat from the meat and cut into 2.5 cm/1 in cubes.

2 In a bowl, mix together the lemon juice, yogurt, salt, 1 crushed garlic clove and the grated ginger. Add the cubes of lamb and mix into the marinade until well coated. Leave to marinate in the fridge overnight.

3 Heat the oil in a large frying pan and fry the cumin seeds for 2 minutes, or until they begin to splutter. Add the bay leaves and cardamom pods and fry for a further 2 minutes, stirring occasionally.

4 Add the onion and remaining garlic and fry for 5 minutes. Stir in the ground coriander, cumin and chilli powder and fry for 2 minutes.

5 Add the marinated lamb and cook over a medium heat for 5 minutes, stirring occasionally.

6 Add the chopped tomatoes, tomato purée and 150 ml/¼ pint/⅔ cup water. Bring to the boil, then reduce the heat. Cover and simmer gently for about 1–1½ hours, or until the meat is soft and tender. Serve with plain or Pilau rice and garnish with toasted cumin seeds and bay leaves.

Beef Madras

Madras curries originate from southern India and are aromatic, robust and pungent in flavour. You can replace the beef with lamb if you prefer.

Serves 4

INGREDIENTS
900 g/2 lb stewing beef
45 ml/3 tbsp oil
1 large onion, finely chopped
4 cloves
4 green cardamom pods
2 green chillies, finely chopped
2.5 cm/1 in piece fresh root ginger, finely
    chopped
2 garlic cloves, crushed
2 dried red chillies
15 ml/1 tbsp ready-made curry paste
10 ml/2 tsp ground coriander
5 ml/1 tsp ground cumin
2.5 ml/½ tsp salt
150 ml/¼ pint/⅔ cup beef stock
Tomato Rice, to serve
fresh coriander sprigs, to garnish

2 Heat the oil in a large frying pan and fry the onion, cloves and cardamom pods for 5 minutes. Add the fresh green chillies, ginger, garlic and dried chillies and fry for a further 2 minutes.

3 Add the curry paste and fry for about 2 minutes. Add the beef and fry for 5–8 minutes, until all the meat pieces are lightly browned.

1 Using a sharp knife, remove any visible fat and cut the meat into 2.5 cm/1 in cubes.

4 Add the coriander, cumin, salt and stock. Cover and simmer for 1–1½ hours. Serve with Tomato Rice and garnish with coriander sprigs.

COOK'S TIP: To make Tomato Rice, peel and chop 4 tomatoes and add to the cooked rice.

Beef Vindaloo

A fiery hot dish, originally from Goa, this is made using a unique blend of ground hot aromatic spices and vinegar.

Serves 4

INGREDIENTS
15 ml/1 tbsp cumin seeds
4 dried red chillies
5 ml/1 tsp black peppercorns
5 green cardamom pods, seeds only
5 ml/1 tsp fenugreek seeds
5 ml/1 tsp black mustard seeds
2.5 ml/½ tsp salt
2.5 ml/½ tsp demerara sugar
60 ml/4 tbsp white wine vinegar
60 ml/4 tbsp oil
1 large onion, finely chopped
900 g/2 lb stewing beef, cut into 2.5 cm/
　1 in cubes
2.5 cm/1 in piece fresh root ginger,
　finely chopped
1 garlic clove, crushed
10 ml/2 tsp ground coriander
2.5 ml/½ tsp ground turmeric
plain and yellow rice, to serve

1 Put the first 6 spice ingredients into a well-cleaned coffee grinder, or use a pestle and mortar, and grind to a fine powder. Add the salt, sugar and white wine vinegar and mix to a thin paste.

2 Heat 30 ml/2 tbsp of the oil in a large frying pan and fry the onion for 10 minutes. Put the onion and the spice mixture into a food processor or blender and process to a coarse paste.

3 Heat the remaining oil in the frying pan and fry the meat cubes for about 10 minutes until lightly browned. Remove the beef cubes with a slotted spoon and set aside.

4 Add the ginger and garlic to the pan and fry for 2 minutes. Stir in the ground coriander and turmeric and fry for 2 minutes.

5 Add the spice and onion paste and fry over a medium heat for about 5 minutes, stirring occasionally.

6 Return the meat to the pan, together with 300 ml/½ pint/ 1¼ cups water. Cover and simmer gently for 1–1½ hours, or until the meat is tender. Serve with plain and yellow rice.

COOK'S TIP: To make plain and yellow rice, infuse a pinch of saffron in 15 ml/1 tbsp hot water. Stir into half the cooked rice. Mix the yellow rice into the plain rice.

Chick-pea & Spinach Curry

Serve this curry with rice or naan and a yogurt raita or chutney.

Serves 3–4

INGREDIENTS
30 ml/2 tbsp sunflower oil
1 large onion, finely chopped
2 garlic cloves, crushed
2.5 cm/1 in piece of fresh root ginger, peeled
    and finely chopped
1 green chilli, seeded and finely chopped
30 ml/2 tbsp ready-made medium
    curry paste
10 ml/2 tsp ground cumin
5 ml/1 tsp ground turmeric
225 g/8 oz can chopped tomatoes
1 green or red pepper, seeded
    and chopped
300 ml/½ pint/1¼ cups vegetable stock
15 ml/1 tbsp tomato purée
450 g/1 lb fresh spinach
425 g/15 oz can chick-peas, drained
45 ml/3 tbsp chopped fresh coriander
5 ml/1 tsp garam masala (optional)
salt

1 Heat the oil in a large saucepan or flameproof casserole. Add the onion, garlic, ginger and chilli. Cook gently for 5 minutes, or until the onions are softened but not browned.

COOK'S TIP: If using dried chick-peas you will need 115 g/4 oz. Soak them overnight in cold water. Boil rapidly for 10 minutes, then simmer until tender before adding in step 5.

2 Stir in the curry paste, cook for 1 minute more, then add the ground cumin and turmeric and cook gently for 1 minute, stirring constantly so that all the flavours are well blended.

3 Add the chopped tomatoes and pepper to the pan and stir well. Pour in the vegetable stock and stir in the tomato purée. Bring to the boil, lower the heat, cover and simmer for 15 minutes.

4 Remove any coarse stalks from the spinach and wash the leaves thoroughly in several changes of water to remove any grit. Drain and chop the leaves and add them to the pan in small batches.

5 Add the chick-peas, cover and cook gently for 5 minutes more. Stir in the fresh coriander, season with salt and sprinkle with garam masala, if using. Serve at once.

Spicy Dhal

Serve with rice, chapatis or naan bread and whatever main dish you like. Try hard-boiled eggs, fried aubergines or even fried mushrooms.

Serves 4–6

INGREDIENTS
225 g/8 oz/1 cup yellow split peas
2 onions, chopped
1 large bay leaf
600 ml/1 pint/2½ cups unsalted stock or water
10 ml/2 tsp black mustard seeds
30 ml/2 tbsp melted butter
1 garlic clove, crushed
2.5 cm/1 in piece fresh root ginger, grated
1 small green pepper, sliced
5 ml/1 tsp ground turmeric
5 ml/1 tsp garam masala or mild
    curry powder
3 tomatoes, peeled and chopped
salt and freshly ground black pepper
fresh coriander or parsley, to garnish

1 Put the split peas, 1 onion and the bay leaf in the stock or water in a covered pan. Simmer for 25 minutes, seasoning lightly towards the end.

2 In a separate pan, fry the mustard seeds in the butter for about 30 seconds, until they start to pop. Add the remaining onion, the garlic, ginger and green pepper.

3 Sauté for about 5 minutes until softened, then stir in the remaining spices and fry for a few seconds more.

4 Add the peas, tomatoes, and a little water if needed. Simmer, covered, for 10 minutes. Garnish and serve.

Chilli Okra

Sometimes okra in restaurants is soggy because it has been left standing.
When you make this dish yourself, you will realize how delicious it is.

Serves 4

INGREDIENTS
350 g/12 oz okra
2 small onions
2 garlic cloves, crushed
1 cm/½ in piece fresh root ginger
1 green chilli, seeded
10 ml/2 tsp ground cumin
10 ml/2 tsp ground coriander
30 ml/2 tbsp vegetable oil
juice of 1 lemon

1 Trim the okra and cut into 1 cm/
½ in lengths. Roughly chop one of
the onions and place in a food
processor or blender with the garlic,
ginger, chilli and 90 ml/6 tbsp water.

2 Process to a paste. Add the cumin
and coriander and process again.

3 Thinly slice the remaining onion
into half rings and fry in the oil for
6–8 minutes, until golden brown.
Transfer to a plate, using a slotted
spoon, and set aside.

4 Reduce the heat and add the garlic
and ginger mixture. Cook for
about 2–3 minutes, stirring frequently,
and then add the okra, lemon juice
and 105 ml/7 tbsp water. Stir well,
cover and simmer over a low heat for
about 10 minutes, until tender. Transfer
to a serving dish, sprinkle with the
fried onion rings and serve.

Curried Mushrooms, Peas & Indian Cheese

Paneer is a traditional cheese made from rich milk. In India, this dish is often eaten with paratha (a deep-fried bread).

Serves 4–6

INGREDIENTS
90 ml/6 tbsp ghee or vegetable oil
225 g/8 oz paneer, cubed
1 onion, finely chopped
a few mint leaves, chopped
50 g/2 oz/½ cup coriander leaves, chopped
3 green chillies, chopped
3 cloves garlic
2.5 cm/1 in piece fresh root ginger, sliced
5 ml/1 tsp turmeric
5 ml/1 tsp chilli powder (optional)
5 ml/1 tsp garam masala
225 g/8 oz/3 cups tiny button mushrooms,
    washed and left whole
225 g/8 oz/2 cups frozen peas, thawed
175 ml/6 fl oz/¾ cup natural yogurt, mixed
    with 5 ml/1 tsp cornflour
salt
mint leaves, to garnish

2 Remove the fried cheese and drain on kitchen paper. Set aside. Grind the onion, mint, coriander, chillies, garlic and ginger in a mortar with a pestle or process in a food processor to a fairly smooth paste. Add to the pan and mix in the turmeric, chilli powder if using, garam masala and salt.

3 Remove the excess ghee or oil from the pan leaving about 15 ml/ 1 tbsp. Heat and fry the paste until the raw onion smell disappears and the oil separates. Transfer to a saucepan.

1 Heat the ghee or oil in a frying pan and fry the paneer cubes until they are golden brown on all sides.

4 Add the mushrooms, peas and paneer. Mix well. Cool the mixture and gradually fold in the yogurt. Simmer for about 10 minutes. Garnish with mint leaves and serve hot.

COOK'S TIP: The addition of cornflour to the yogurt helps it to blend without curdling.

49

Aloo Gobi

Cauliflower and potatoes are encrusted with aromatic Indian spices and then fried in this delicious recipe.

Serves 4

INGREDIENTS
450 g/1 lb potatoes, cut into 2.5 cm/1 in
   chunks
30 ml/2 tbsp oil
5 ml/1 tsp cumin seeds
1 green chilli, finely chopped
450 g/1 lb cauliflower, broken into florets
5 ml/1 tsp ground coriander
5 ml/1 tsp ground cumin
1.5 ml/¼ tsp chilli powder
2.5 ml/½ tsp ground turmeric
2.5 ml/½ tsp salt
chopped fresh coriander, to garnish
tomato and onion salad and pickle, to serve

1 Par-boil the potatoes in a large saucepan of boiling water for 10 minutes. Drain well and set aside.

2 Heat the oil in a large frying pan and fry the cumin seeds for about 2 minutes, until they begin to splutter. Add the green chilli and fry for a further 1 minute.

3 Add the cauliflower florets and fry, stirring, for 5 minutes.

4 Add the potatoes, the ground spices and salt and cook for 7–10 minutes, until the vegetables are tender. Garnish with coriander and serve with tomato and onion salad and pickle.

COOK'S TIP: For tomato and onion salad, mix sliced tomatoes and onions with a chopped green chilli. Add lemon juice, salt and pepper and serve with grated coconut.

Pilau Rice with Whole Spices

This colourful and fragrant rice dish makes a perfect accompaniment to a special Indian meal.

Serves 4–6

INGREDIENTS
generous pinch of saffron strands
600 ml/1 pint/2½ cups hot chicken stock
50 g/2 oz/4 tbsp butter
1 onion, chopped
1 garlic clove, crushed
½ cinnamon stick
6 cardamoms
1 bay leaf
250 g/9 oz/1¼ cups basmati rice, rinsed
   and drained
50 g/2 oz/⅓ cup sultanas
15 ml/1 tbsp oil
50 g/2 oz/⅓ cup cashew nuts

1 Soak the saffron in the hot stock. Heat the butter in a saucepan and fry the onion and garlic for 5 minutes. Add the cinnamon stick, cardamoms and bay leaf and cook for 2 minutes.

2 Add the rice and cook, stirring, for 2 minutes. Pour in the stock and add the sultanas. Bring to the boil, stir, then lower the heat, cover and cook for 15 minutes, or until the rice is tender and the liquid absorbed.

3 Meanwhile, fry the cashew nuts in the oil until browned. Drain and serve scattered over the rice.

Mango Chutney

Chutneys are usually served as an accompaniment to curry, but this one is particularly nice served as a dip with poppadums.

Makes 450 g/1 lb/2 cups

INGREDIENTS
50 ml/2 fl oz/¼ cup malt vinegar
2.5 ml/½ tsp dried chillies, crushed
6 whole cloves
6 whole peppercorns
5 ml/1 tsp roasted cumin seeds
2.5 ml/½ tsp onion seeds
175 g/6 oz/¾ cup sugar
450 g/1 lb unripe mangoes, peeled and cubed
5 cm/2 in piece fresh root ginger,
   finely sliced
2 cloves garlic, crushed
thin rind of 1 orange or lemon (optional)
salt

1 In a large, heavy-based saucepan, heat the vinegar with the chillies, cloves, peppercorns, cumin and onion seeds, salt and sugar. Simmer gently over a low heat for about 15 minutes, until the flavours of the spices infuse into the vinegar.

2 Add the mangoes, ginger, garlic and rind, if using. Simmer until the mango is soft and mushy and most of the vinegar has evaporated.

3 Cool the mixture and pour into sterilized bottles. Leave in the fridge for a few days before serving.

Hot Lime Pickle

A good lime pickle is not only delicious served with any meal, but it also increases the appetite and aids digestion.

Makes 450 g/1 lb/2 cups

INGREDIENTS
25 limes
225 g/8 oz salt
50 g/2 oz/½ cup ground fenugreek
50 g/2 oz/½ cup mustard powder
150 g/5 oz/1¼ cups chilli powder
15 g/½ oz/2 tbsp turmeric
600 ml/1 pint/2½ cups mustard oil
5 ml/1 tsp asafoetida
25 g/1 oz/2 tbsp yellow mustard
   seeds, crushed

1 Cut each lime into 8 pieces and remove the seeds. Place the limes in a large sterilized jar or glass bowl.

2 Add the salt and toss with the limes. Cover and leave in a warm place until they become soft and dull brown in colour, for 1 to 2 weeks.

3 Mix together the spices and add to the limes. Cover and leave in a warm place for a further 2 or 3 days.

4 Heat the mustard oil in a frying pan and fry the asafoetida and mustard seeds until they begin to pop. When the oil reaches smoking point, pour it over the limes. Mix well, cover with a clean cloth and leave in a warm place for about 1 week before serving.

Sweet-&-sour Raita

Raitas are traditionally served with most meals as accompaniments that are cooling to the palate.

Serves 4

INGREDIENTS
475 ml/16 fl oz/2 cups natural yogurt
5 ml/1 tsp salt
5 ml/1 tsp sugar
30 ml/2 tbsp clear honey
7.5 ml/1½ tsp mint sauce
30 ml/2 tbsp roughly chopped
   fresh coriander
1 green chilli, seeded and finely chopped
1 medium onion, diced
50 ml/2 fl oz/¼ cup water

1 Pour the yogurt into a bowl and whisk it well. Add the salt, sugar, honey and mint sauce.

2 Reserve a little coriander for the garnish and add the rest to the yogurt mixture. Stir in the chilli, onion and water.

3 Taste the raita to check the sweetness and stir in a little more honey, if desired.

4 Whisk once again and pour into a serving bowl. Garnish with the reserved coriander and place in the fridge until ready to serve.

COOK'S TIP: Grated cucumber can also be added to this recipe.

Chapati

Chapatis are prepared daily in most Indian homes.

Makes 10–12

INGREDIENTS
350 g/12 oz/3 cups *chana atta* flour
5 ml/1 tsp salt
water, to mix
a few drops of vegetable oil,
    for brushing
50 g/2 oz/½ cup *chana atta* flour, for dusting
ghee or unsalted butter, for spreading

1 Sift the flour and salt into a large bowl. Make a well in the centre and gradually add small quantities of water until you have a smooth but pliable dough. Grease the palms of your hands and knead the dough well. Keep the dough covered until you are ready to use it.

2 Divide the dough into 10–12 equal portions, using one portion at a time and keeping the rest covered. Knead each portion into a ball, then flatten with your hands and place on a floured surface. Roll out until you have a circle about 18 cm/7 in in diameter.

3 Heat a heavy griddle and, when hot, roast the chapatis on each side, pressing the edges down gently with a spatula. When both sides are cooked, brush the upper side lightly with ghee or unsalted butter.

Naan

Traditionally, naan is baked in a tandoor or clay oven.

Makes 6–8

INGREDIENTS
10 ml/2 tsp easy-blend yeast
60 ml/4 tbsp warm milk
10 ml/2 tsp sugar
450 g/1 lb plain flour
5 ml/1 tsp baking powder
2.5 ml/½ tsp salt
150 ml/¼ pint/⅔ cup milk
150 ml/¼ pint/⅔ cup natural yogurt, beaten
1 egg, beaten
25 g/1 oz/2 tbsp ghee, melted
flour, for dusting
chopped coriander leaves and onion
    seeds, to sprinkle
ghee, for greasing

1 Mix the yeast, warm milk and sugar and leave to become frothy. Sift together the flour, baking powder and salt. Fold in the yeast mixture, milk, yogurt, egg and ghee.

2 Knead the dough. Cover and keep in a warm place until it doubles and springs back to the touch. Preheat the oven to 200°C/400°F/Gas 6.

3 Roll out the dough on a floured surface. Make each naan about 25 cm/10 in long and 15 cm/6 in wide. Sprinkle with the coriander and onion seeds. Place on greased trays and bake until flecked with brown.

Mango Sorbet with Sauce

After a heavy meal, this makes a very refreshing dessert. Mango is said to be one of the oldest fruits cultivated in India.

Serves 4–6

INGREDIENTS
900 g/2 lb mango pulp
2.5 ml/½ tsp lemon juice
grated rind of 1 orange and 1 lemon
4 egg whites, whisked until peaks form
50 g/2 oz/¼ cup caster sugar
120 ml/4 fl oz/½ cup double cream
50 g/2 oz/½ cup icing sugar

1 In a large, chilled bowl, mix 425 g/
15 oz of the mango pulp with the
lemon juice and the rind.

2 Gently fold in the egg whites and
caster sugar. Cover with clear film
and place in the freezer for at least
1 hour until beginning to set.

3 Remove the bowl from the freezer
and beat the contents. Transfer to
an ice cream container and freeze until
fully set. Scrape the ice crystals from
the side of the bowl and whisk the
mixture to break down the crystals.

4 Whip the double cream with the
icing sugar and the remaining
mango pulp. Chill the sauce for 24
hours. Remove the sorbet from the
freezer 10 minutes before serving.
Scoop out individual servings and
cover with a generous helping of
mango sauce. Serve immediately.

Kulfi

Kulfi-wallahs have always made kulfi – ice cream – without using modern freezers. It is packed into metal cones, sealed and churned until set.

Serves 4–6

INGREDIENTS
3 x 400 ml/14 fl oz cans evaporated milk
3 egg whites, whisked until peaks form
350 g/12 oz/3 cups icing sugar
5 ml/1 tsp cardamom powder
15 ml/1 tbsp rose water
175 g/6 oz/1½ cups pistachios, chopped
75 g/3 oz/½ cup sultanas
75 g/3 oz/¾ cup flaked almonds
25 g/1 oz/3 tbsp glacé cherries, halved

1 Remove the labels from the cans of milk and lay the cans in a pan with a tight lid. Fill the pan with enough water to reach three-quarters of the way up the cans. Bring to the boil.

2 Cover and simmer for 20 minutes. Cool, remove and chill the cans in the fridge for 24 hours.

3 Empty the milk into a large, chilled freezerproof bowl. Whisk until it doubles in quantity, then fold in the whisked egg whites and icing sugar.

4 Gently fold in the remaining ingredients, seal the bowl with clear film and freeze for 1 hour.

5 Remove the ice cream from the freezer and mix well with a fork. Transfer to a serving container and freeze again. Remove from the freezer 10 minutes before serving.

Indian Fruit Salad

This is a very appetizing and refreshing salad, with a typically Indian combination of citrus fruits seasoned with salt and pepper.

Serves 6

INGREDIENTS
115 g/4 oz/1 cup seedless green and
   black grapes
225 g/8 oz canned mandarin segments,
   drained
2 navel oranges, peeled and segmented
225 g/8 oz canned grapefruit segments,
   drained
balls from 1 honeydew melon
balls from ½ watermelon
1 fresh mango, peeled and sliced
juice of 1 lemon
2.5 ml/½ tsp sugar
1.5 ml/¼ tsp freshly ground
   cumin seeds
salt and freshly ground black pepper

1 Place all the fruit in a large serving bowl and add the lemon juice. Toss gently to prevent breaking up the fruit.

2 Mix together the remaining ingredients and sprinkle over the fruit. Gently toss once more, chill thoroughly and serve.

Rice Pudding

A rich and creamy dessert infused with spices.

Serves 4–6

INGREDIENTS
15 ml/1 tbsp ghee
5 cm/2 in piece cinnamon stick
175 g/6 oz/¾ cup brown sugar
115 g/4 oz/⅔ cup coarsely-ground rice
1.2 litres/2 pints/5 cups milk
5 ml/1 tsp ground cardamom
50 g/2 oz/⅓ cup sultanas
25 g/1 oz/¼ cup flaked almonds
2.5 ml/½ tsp freshly-ground nutmeg, to serve

1 In a heavy pan, melt the ghee and fry the cinnamon and sugar. Keep frying until the sugar begins to caramelize. Reduce the heat immediately when this happens.

2 Add the rice and half the milk. Bring to the boil, stirring constantly to avoid the milk boiling over. Reduce the heat and simmer until the rice is cooked, stirring frequently.

3 Add the remaining milk, cardamom, sultanas and almonds and simmer, but keep stirring to prevent the rice from sticking to the base of the pan. When the mixture has thickened, serve hot or cold, sprinkled with the nutmeg.

Vermicelli Pudding

A dessert for nut lovers, sweetened with dried fruit.

Serves 4–6

INGREDIENTS
90 ml/6 tbsp ghee
115 g/4 oz vermicelli, coarsely broken
25 g/1 oz/¼ cup flaked almonds
25 g/1 oz/¼ cup pistachios, slivered
25 g/1 oz/¼ cup hazelnuts
50 g/2 oz/⅓ cup sultanas
50 g/2 oz/⅓ cup dates, stoned and slivered
1.2 litres/2 pints/5 cups milk
60 ml/4 tbsp dark brown sugar
1 sachet saffron powder

1 Heat 60 ml/4 tbsp of the ghee in a frying pan and sauté the vermicelli until golden brown. (If you are using the Italian variety, sauté it a little longer.) Remove and keep aside.

2 Heat the remaining ghee and fry the nuts, sultanas and dates until the sultanas swell. Add to the vermicelli.

3 Heat the milk in a large heavy pan and add the sugar. Bring to the boil, add the vermicelli mixture and boil, stirring constantly. Reduce the heat and simmer until the vermicelli is soft and you have a fairly thick pudding. Fold in the saffron powder and serve hot or cold.

Index

Aloo Gobi, 50-1

Balti Chicken, 34-5
Balti Prawns in Hot
  Sauce, 28-9
Beef: Beef Madras,
  40-1
  Beef Vindaloo, 42-3
  Kofta, 13
Biryani, Chicken,
  36-7
Breads, 56-7

Cauliflower: Aloo
  Gobi, 50-1
  Spiced Cauliflower
  Soup, 18
Chapati, 56-7
Chick-pea & Spinach
  Curry, 44-5
Chicken: Balti
  Chicken, 34-5
  Chicken Biryani,
  36-7
  Chicken Korma,
  32-3
  Chicken Tikka, 12
  Tandoori Chicken,
  30-1

Chillies, 8
Chilli Okra, 47
Chutney, Mango, 53
Cod: Fish Stew, 22-3
Curry Powder, 9

Dhal: Dhal Soup, 19

Fish Curry, 20-1
Fish Stew, 22-3
Fruit Salad, Indian, 61

Garam Masala, 9
Goan-style Mussels,
  26-7

Ice cream: Kulfi, 60

Kofta, 13
Kulfi, 60

Lamb: Curried Lamb
  Samosas, 10-11
  Rogan Josh, 38-9
Lentils: Dhal Soup, 19
  Spicy Dhal, 46
Lime Pickle, Hot, 54

Mangoes: Mango
  Chutney, 53
  Mango Sorbet with
  Sauce, 58-9
Mushrooms: Curried
  Mushrooms, Peas &
  Indian Cheese,
  48-9
Mussels, Goan-style,
  26-7

Naan, 56-7

Okra, Chilli, 47
Onion Bhajias, 14-15

Pilau Rice with
  Whole Spices, 52
Potatoes: Aloo Gobi,
  50-1
Prawns: Balti Prawns
  in Hot Sauce, 28-9
  King Prawn
  Korma, 24-5

Raita, Sweet-&-
  sour, 55
Rice: Chicken
  Biryani, 36-7

Pilau Rice with
  Whole Spices, 52
Rice Pudding, 62-3
Rogan Josh, 38-9

Samosas, Curried
  Lamb, 10-11
Sorbet, Mango, 58-9
Soups, 16-19
Spices, 6-7
  crushing, 8
  Curry Powder, 9
  Garam Masala, 9
Sweet-&-sour
  Raita, 55

Tandoori Chicken,
  30-1
Tomato & Coriander
  Soup, 16-17

Vermicelli Pudding,
  62-3

Yogurt: Sweet-&-
  sour Raita, 55

This edition is published by Hermes House

© Anness Publishing Limited 1999, updated 2001, 2002.

Hermes House is an imprint of Anness Publishing Limited,
Hermes House, 88–89 Blackfriars Road, London SE1 8HA

Publisher: Joanna Lorenz
Editor: Valerie Ferguson
Series Designer: Bobbie Colgate Stone
Designer: Andrew Heath
Editorial Reader: Hayley Kerr
Production Controller: Joanna King

Recipes contributed by: Roz Denny, Rafi Fernandez,
Sarah Gates, Shehzad Husain, Christine Ingram,
Manisha Kanani, Lesley Mackley, Sue Maggs,
Maggie Pannell, Liz Trigg.

Photography: Karl Adamson, Edward Allwright,
David Armstrong, Steve Baxter, Michelle Garrett,
Ferguson Hill, David Jordan.

Notes:
For all recipes, quantities are given in both metric and
imperial measures and, where appropriate, measures
are also given in standard cups and spoons.
Follow one set, but not a mixture, because they are
not interchangeable.

Standard spoon and cup measures are level.

1 tsp = 5 ml   1 tbsp = 15 ml   1 cup = 250 ml/8 fl oz

Australian standard tablespoons are 20 ml.
Australian readers should use 3 tsp in place of 1 tbsp
for measuring small quantities of gelatine,
cornflour, salt, etc.

Medium eggs are used unless otherwise stated.

3 5 7 9 10 8 6 4

Printed in China